Table of Cont

MW01051344

Essential Question

What can different cultures teach us?

Tales
to Live By

Tales to Live By

Student Objectives

I will be able to:

- Read and analyze tales from different cultures that teach lessons.

- Share ideas with my peers.

- Build my vocabulary knowledge.

- Write informational, narrative, and opinion texts.

Credits
Editor: Cindy Peattie
Creative Director: Laurie Berger
Art Directors: Melody DeJesus, Kathryn DelVecchio-Kempa, Doug McGredy, Chris Moroch
Production: Kosta Triantafillis
Director of Photography: Doug Schneider
Photo Assistant: Jackie Friedman

Illustrations: Alexander Honore: p. 2; Gerald Kelley: p. 3 (top); Jaqueline Rogers p. 3 (bottom); juanbjuan Oliver: p. 4; Stephen Stone: p. 5; Gerardo Suzan: p. 6-9; Kirk Parish: p. 10-13; Daniela Dogliani: p. 16; Fermin Solis: p. 17; David Harrington: p. 18-25; Lisa Manusak: p. 28; Roger Simo: p. 29; Mariano Epelbaum p. 30-37

Printed in Mexico. 10789/0122/102769

ISBN: 978-1-4900-9186-0

Tips for Text Annotation

As you read closely for different purposes, remember to annotate the text. Use the symbols below to annotate.

Symbol	Purpose
underline	Identify a key detail.
☆	Star an important idea in the margin.
① ② ③	Record a sequence of events.
jealous	Circle a key word or phrase.
?	Mark a place in the text where you have a question. Write your question in the margin.
!	Mark a place in the text where you have an idea. Write your idea or thought in the margin.

Your annotations might look like this.

Notes	
	① Many moons ago, there lived a (brave) warrior. He was called the Invisible One. ☆ No one could see him except his sister. <u>He pledged to marry the first woman who could see him.</u>
What does the word callous mean? I wonder why she was called Rough-Face Girl.	② Nearby, there lived a man with two daughters. The elder daughter was callous and cruel. The younger, called Rough-Face Girl, was gentle and kind. Rough-Face Girl worked hard. She tended the fire. It made her face rough and chapped. Her idle sister did nothing.
	③ One day, Idle Sister announced, "I want to marry the Invisible One!" She hurried

LEXILE® is a trademark of MetaMetrics, Inc., and is registered in the United States and abroad.

E-book and digital teacher's guide available at benchmarkuniverse.com.

BENCHMARK EDUCATION COMPANY
145 Huguenot Street • New Rochelle, NY • 10801

Toll-Free 1-877-236-2465
www.benchmarkeducation.com
www.benchmarkuniverse.com

Remember to annotate as you read.

Notes

The Best Idea

1 Once there was a meeting of the mice to discuss their problem with Cat. The cat was so sneaky that he could pounce before the mice knew he was around!

2 Young Mouse had an idea. "Let's hang a bell on his neck. Then we will hear him coming and have time to scoot away!" The mice cheered and agreed it was the best idea they had ever heard.

3 Then Old Mouse asked a question. "Who will put the bell on the cat?"

4 No one answered. It was not such a good idea after all.

The Size of Kindness

1   Long ago, Ant and Elephant were both the same size, which was about the size of a horse. One day they found a girl who was hurt and could not walk. "Please, may I ride on your back?" she asked.

2   Ant complained, "No, that would not be comfortable for me!"

3   Elephant, however, helped the girl onto his back and took her home. As a reward, the girl's father gave Elephant and Ant each a gift based on the size of their kindness. Elephant became large and mighty, while Ant became small.

Remember to annotate as you read.

Notes

Why the Sky Is Far Away

1   Many years ago, the sky was very close to our Earth. People could reach up, break off a piece of the sky, and eat it! The delicious sky tasted like coconuts, strawberries, and other scrumptious foods. Since people didn't work for their food, they spent time painting beautiful pictures, weaving colorful cloths, and singing songs.

2   However, the people often wasted the sky's food, taking much more than they needed. Soon heaps of leftover food were piled everywhere.

3   The sky became very angry, and spoke to the people. "You are wasting my precious gift of food. If you continue to do that, I will go away!"

4   For a short time, the people were careful. They took only what they needed from the sky. However, one day, during a lively festival, they forgot all about the sky's warning.

5   The people danced and sang and ate. They broke off huge pieces of the sky. It was much more than they could ever eat.

6   Some people concealed their leftovers by burying them. However, the sky saw everything and said, "You are greedy and wasteful. Now I will go far away."

7   "But how will we eat?" asked the people.

8   "You will work for your food by planting crops," the sky replied. Then the sky floated up high, where it is today.

King Midas

1   Long ago, there lived a king named Midas who was the richest man in the land. The king was fond of gold and loved it more than anything, except his daughter, Marigold.

2   One day, as King Midas counted his coins, a stranger appeared. "If I could grant you one wish, what would it be?" he asked.

3   "I'd wish that everything I touched turned into gold," King Midas replied.

4   "Your wish is granted!" exclaimed the stranger. "When you awake tomorrow, you'll have that power."

5   The next morning, the king awoke earlier than usual. He walked around the palace, touching every object. He was delighted and thrilled when everything he touched became gold!

6   However, when he stopped to take a sip of water, the glass of water turned to gold! Then Marigold ran to him. But when he embraced her with a kiss, she became a golden statue!

7   "What have I done?" the king cried. And he wept with grief and sorrow.

8   Suddenly, the stranger appeared before him.

9   "You look like the saddest man in the land," said the stranger.

10   "I've lost everything I care about," sobbed the king.

11   "Fill this pitcher with water from the lake," instructed the stranger. "Then sprinkle it on everything you've turned into gold."

12   King Midas followed his instructions. When everything returned to normal, the king was the happiest man ever!

Mercury and the Ax

1   A young man went to the forest to chop down a tree. It was June and the hot noon sun beat down on him. His hands started to sweat. The ax flew out of his loose hands and landed in the river. The man began to cry. "My ax might not have been new, but it was all I had. It is lost forever!"

2   Mercury, the god, rose out of the river. "I will help you," he said. He dived deep into the river. Soon he came back with a golden ax. "Is this your ax?" he asked.

3   "No," said the young man.

4   So Mercury dived into the river a second time. He came back with a silver ax. "Is this your ax?" he asked.

5   "No," said the young man.

6   So Mercury dived into the river a third time. He came back with the young man's old, wooden ax. "Is this your ax?" he asked.

7   "It is!" yelled the young man. "Thank you."

8   "Young man," said Mercury, "you told the truth instead of being greedy. Because you were honest, I will give you the golden and silver axes, too. Enjoy!"

BuildReflectWrite

Build Knowledge

Compare and contrast "Why the Sky Is Far Away" and "King Midas." Use a Venn diagram to identify how the characters and lessons in both texts are similar and different.

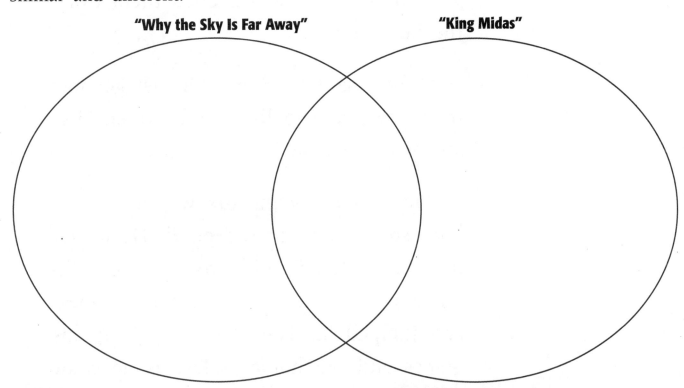

"Why the Sky Is Far Away"   "King Midas"

Reflect

What can different cultures teach us?

Based on this week's texts, write new ideas and questions you have about the essential question.

_____

_____

_____

_____

_____

_____

Write to Sources

Informative/Explanatory

In "Why the Sky Is Far Away" and "King Midas," the main characters are both greedy and learn lessons. Write a short essay in which you compare the main characters' greed and lessons learned. Use story events from the reading selections as the basis of your explanation.

Remember to annotate as you read.

Notes

Fox Gets Tricked

1   A young boy was enjoying a large bunch of grapes. Fox saw the grapes and wanted them so he snatched them from the boy's hands.

2   "Fine," said the boy. "I'll just get more from the fox who lives underwater. His are better anyway."

3   The boy knew the fox would follow him, so he went to the pond. He looked into the water. So did Fox, who saw his reflection. Fox dropped the boy's grapes and jumped in. The boy scooped up his grapes and ran home as fast as he could!

The Lion and the Man

1   Once upon a time there was a lion and a man arguing about who was the mightiest.

2   Man suggested they travel to a city where an answer might be found. Lion agreed and they traveled to the city center where they saw a statue. The statue showed a mighty warrior standing over the slain body of a lion. "This is proof," Man said.

3   Lion laughed. "That statue was made by a man! It would have been quite a different scene if a lion had made it. Truth often belongs to the one telling the story."

Notes

A Foxy Garden

by Jeffrey Fuerst

1   One July day when pleasant smells surfed along the breeze, Bear found a row of ripe blueberry bushes by the creek. He stuffed himself with berries and then fell asleep. Squirrel and Rabbit followed their noses to the blueberry patch, too. When they started eating the berries, Bear woke up.

2   "Hey!" growled Bear. "Those are MY blueberries. Scram, or else!"

3   Squirrel and Rabbit hightailed it back to the woods where they told their wise friend Fox what happened. "Bear is being his usual selfish self," said Fox. "We'll have to do something about that."

Notes

4   Fox grabbed a handful of his special, fast-growing seeds. Then he went to Bear and said, "I am going to plant a garden with delicious vegetables. I could use someone strong to help."

5   "What's in it for me?" asked Bear as he gulped down another pawful of berries.

6   "We'll share, of course," said Fox. "You can have everything that grows above the ground. I will get everything that grows below the ground."

7   Bear laughed. "You will eat stuff covered in dirt? Yuck! I will take that deal."

8   "How about we grow carrots?" Fox suggested.

Notes

9   Bear thought for a moment and then said, "I love carrots. They are good raw or cooked. Let's get to work."

10   Bear and Fox dug holes for the carrot seeds. They planted and watered the seeds. The seeds grew. After a while, the carrots were ready.

11   Bear pulled up the carrots, his mouth watering at the thought of carrot soup and carrot cake. Fox took the carrots, cut off the green tops, and gave them to Bear. Fox kept the orange roots for himself.

12   "Hey!" said Bear. "The green tops are not good for eating. I want the orange part."

13   "Ah," said Fox, "the orange part is the root. It grows below the ground. Remember our deal? You got everything that grows above the ground."

14   Bear roared and growled but there was nothing he could do; a deal is a deal. Then he said, "I want to plant a new crop! This time, I will get what grows below the ground. You will get what grows above the ground."

15   "Okay," said Fox. "How about celery?"

16   "I love celery!" said Bear. "It's a tasty snack with peanut butter, and makes a healthful drink, too."

17   Bear and Fox planted and watered the celery seeds. The seeds grew. After a while, the celery was ready.

18   Bear pulled up the celery, licking his lips in anticipation. Fox cut off the thick stems that grew above the ground. "Crispy and refreshing," said Fox as he munched on a stem, giving Bear the celery roots that grew below the ground.

19   "Ugh!" said Bear biting into the bitter celery root. "You fooled me once. You fooled me twice. This time let's plant another garden. I will get the roots and the stems!"

20   "Okay," said Fox. "How about something that makes a good salad?"

21   Bear thought about salad. "Lettuce makes a good salad," he said, his tongue tapping his teeth. "It is good in a sandwich, too. Let's get to work."

22   Bear and Fox planted and watered lettuce seeds. The seeds grew. After a while, the lettuce was ready to harvest.

23   Bear picked armfuls of lettuce. "It's mine, all mine!" he cried.

24   "Not so fast," said Fox. "You said you would get the roots and the stems. What you are holding are the leaves of lettuce. As we agreed, those belong to me."

25   "Unfair!" yelled Bear. "Unfair, unfair, unfair! And now I am hungry for lettuce. I want a salad with carrots and celery."

26   "What a good idea, Bear," said Fox. "I will make a lettuce, carrot, and celery salad. I will invite Squirrel and Rabbit. The three of us will have a picnic under the chestnut tree."

27   Bear stormed off to the blueberry bushes by the creek. "Unfair," he muttered, slowly nibbling a berry. Soon, sadness pushed aside anger, for now Bear felt left out. He listened to the creek flowing past him.

Notes

28   "*Gurgle, whoosh,*" said the creek and Bear understood. He took a long, cool drink. Then he picked four baskets of blueberries and brought them to the picnickers under the chestnut tree.

29   "I was wrong not to share the berries," said Bear. "Here is a basket for each of you."

30   "Why, thank you, Bear," said Squirrel.

31   "They will make a yummy dessert!" said Rabbit.

32   "And since you are sharing," said Fox, "please join our picnic."

The Many Tales of Red Riding Hood

1   Have you heard the tale of Red Riding Hood? Have you read a book about this girl and the Big Bad Wolf? Red Riding Hood is told all over the world. It is told in a different way in each place.

2   In China, kids hear about three girls. They're left at home alone. Their mom tells them to lock the door. But a wolf named Lon Po Po stops by. He is dressed to look like a grandmother. They let him into their home. But the oldest girl catches on to his trick and saves her sisters.

3   In Africa, kids hear about a girl named Pretty Salma. She runs into Big Bad Dog on her way to the market. He tricks her and dresses as her grandmother. With the help of Anansi the spider, she saves the day.

4   In the Cajun tale, the wolf is an alligator. He wants to eat a girl named Petite Rouge, or "Little Red." She and her cat trick the alligator and survive.

5   If you could make up a story about Red Riding Hood, what would you call her? What animal would play the Big Bad Wolf?

BuildReflectWrite

Build Knowledge

Based on your reading, analyze the characters' points of view
in "A Foxy Garden."

Analyzing Characters' Points of View	
How would you describe Fox's point of view?	**How does Bear's point of view change at the end of the story?**

Reflect

What can different cultures teach us?

Based on this week's texts, write new ideas and questions you have about the essential question.

_____

_____

_____

_____

_____

_____

Write to Sources

Narrative

After reading "Why the Sky Is Far Away" and "A Foxy Garden," write a short story about greedy characters who learn to share. Your narrative should include what you learned about the characters from the reading selections.

Remember to annotate as you read.

Notes

A Gift for Mom

1 Mia wanted to give her mom the best birthday present. She hadn't saved money for a gift as her brother, Nat, did. She couldn't draw like her sister, Jess.

2 *What am I good at?* Mia thought to herself. She started to make a list, but soon got lost in writing a story. "That's it!" Mia said. "I can write!"

3 Mia wrote a really funny story about a mom who lived in a jungle with wild birds named Mia, Nat, and Jess.

4 Mom laughed and laughed. "Thank you, Mia! Laughter is the best gift of all!"

Try, Try Again

by T. H. Palmer

It's a lesson you should heed,
Try, try again.
If at first you don't succeed,
Try, try again.

Once or twice though you should fail,
Try, try again.
If you would at last prevail,
Try, try again;
If we strive, it's no disgrace
Though we do not win the race;
What should you do in that case?
Try, try again.

Remember to annotate as you read.

Notes

On One Wheel

by Carly Schuna

1   I tried to move, but it was too late. *Thwack!* The ball smacked me in the knee.

2   "Ouch," I groaned.

3   Laughter echoed off the walls of the gym. I sighed. Sports are not my thing. Well, normal sports are not my thing, anyway. Maybe making friends at my new school would be tougher than I thought . . .

4   "You're out, Casey!" said Martha. "Make room for those of us who can play."

5   I leaned up against the wall and watched the rest of the game. During the next round, I actually dodged the ball—but then I stumbled and fell down.

6   I heard giggles all around, and then I saw Ms. Perkins standing over me.

7   "Casey, are you okay?" she asked.

8   "My knee hurts," I said.

9   Ms. Perkins helped me up. "Do you know where the nurse's office is?" she asked.

10   I shook my head.

11   "Martha, please take Casey to the nurse," said Ms. Perkins.

12 "So, you're not a dodgeball player," said Martha as we walked down the hall. "What are you good at?"

13 "Well," I admitted, "I'm just not very good at normal sports."

14 Martha snorted. "That's for sure," she said.

15 The nurse put an ice pack on my knee and told me to lie down.

16 I stared at the ceiling and remembered what Martha had said in the hallway. How was I going to make friends if I couldn't even play the sports we did in gym class?

17   "Mom," I said as I got into the car later, "I can't do anything!"

18   "What do you mean?" asked Mom.

19   "Martha says I can't play dodgeball. She's kind of right."

20   Mom frowned. "Sweetie, you can do lots of things."

21   "Not dodgeball."

22   "Dodgeball takes practice," said Mom. "You're good at lots of things. You can sing, you can fold origami, and you can unicycle!"

23   I looked at Mom. "Hmm," I said.

24   "You're the only kid at unicycle club who can wheel walk," Mom added. "You're better than the grown-ups!"

25   Mom was right—I am awesome on the unicycle. I can do lots of fun tricks.

26   At home, my knee felt better, and Mom let me take my unicycle out to the driveway and practice some tricks. I did a hop twist and a seat drop. A couple of cars honked at me, and one driver even poked his head out the window and said, "Nice job!"

27   That night, I had a dream. It was gym class, and we were playing basketball. Instead of throwing balls at the basket, though, everyone was throwing them at me. Balls pummeled me from all sides, and everybody was laughing really loudly.

28   Then my unicycle flew down from the sky. I hopped on it, scooped up a ball, dribbled around the gym, and made a slam dunk.

Notes

29   I woke up with an idea. "Can I ride my unicycle to school today?" I asked Mom at breakfast.

30   She poured me some orange juice. "Hmm," she said. "I think that's okay, if I ride my bike next to you."

31   "Yes!" I said.

32   The sidewalk leading to school is uneven, but I didn't fall once. I even wheel walked for part of the way. When we got close to school, kids started staring at me.

33   "Whoa!" somebody said. "You can ride a unicycle?"

34   Then I saw Martha looking right at me. I hopped off my unicycle.

35   "What is that?" asked Martha. "Did you lose half your bike or something?"

36   "Not exactly," I said. "This is my unicycle. I ride with a club. Sometimes we even perform at fairs. I've done it since I was five."

37   "Can I try?" asked Martha.

38   I looked at Mom. She nodded.

39   Mom stood on one side of the unicycle and helped Martha up. I stood on the other side and let Martha grasp my arm. A crowd of kids gathered.

40   Martha tried to pedal forward, but she fell off the unicycle right away. A couple of kids snickered.

41   Martha looked at me, but I didn't laugh. "It's hard," I said. "Want to try again?"

42   Martha nodded. We helped her up and she fell off again.

43   More kids laughed. "That's not nice," I said. "She's trying!"

44   Martha looked at me. "Can I see you do it again?" she asked.

45   "Sure!" I said. I hopped on my unicycle and zoomed around forward and backward. Then I took my feet off the pedals and did my wheel walk.

46   When I dismounted, everybody clapped. Mom grinned at me and said, "Nice job!"

47   "You're pretty good at that," said Martha.

48   "Better than at dodgeball," I said.

49   Martha giggled, and I grinned. Maybe making friends wouldn't be so bad after all.

No Small Trick

1 My name is Paul. I go to a special school in the city. We have kids from all over the world. After lunch, we like to do one thing: Play ball.

2 "Where's the soccer ball?" I asked.

3 "All we have is this ball," said Yosef, "a basketball."

4 I looked over at Carlos. He's a new kid in our class. He came here from Spain. He's not very tall, but he's the best soccer player in school.

5 I tossed the ball to Carlos. He caught it with one hand. And you won't believe what I saw next! Carlos put the ball on the tip of his finger. Then he spun the ball around and around. He walked in a circle with the ball spinning faster and faster. Then he dribbled the ball, stopped, and launched it into the basket. *Swish!* My jaw dropped open. "How did you learn to do that?" I asked. "Talk about talent! I thought you only knew how to play soccer."

6 Carlos smiled. "My mom played basketball in college. We play together on the weekends. Would you like to learn a trick?"

7 "Just a small, simple one," I said. "I'm only a beginner."

BuildReflectWrite

Build Knowledge

Based on reading "On One Wheel," identify each character's point of view and the lesson they learn.

Character	Point of View	Lesson Learned
Casey		
Martha		

Reflect

What can different cultures teach us?

Based on this week's texts, write new ideas and questions you have about the essential question.

_____

_____

_____

_____

_____

Write to Sources

Opinion

After reading "On One Wheel," reread "A Foxy Garden." Both stories have characters that learn lessons. Choose one character from each story and write a short essay that explains why you think these characters needed to learn a lesson. Use evidence from both texts to support your opinion and reasons.

Support for Collaborative Conversation

Discussion Prompts

Share a new idea or opinion . . .

I think that _____.

I notice that _____.

My opinion is _____.

An important event was when _____.

Gain the floor . . .

I would like to add _____.

Excuse me for interrupting, but _____.

That made me think of _____.

Build on a peer's idea or opinion . . .

I also think that _____.

In addition, _____.

Another idea is _____.

Express agreement with a peer's idea . . .

I agree with [Name] because _____.

I agree that _____.

I think that is important because _____.

Respectfully express disagreement . . .

I disagree with [Name] because _____.

I understand your point of view, but I think _____.

Have you considered that _____?

Ask a clarifying question . . .

What did you mean when you said _____?

Are you saying that _____?

Can you explain what you mean by _____?

Clarify for others . . .

I meant that _____.

I am trying to say that _____.

Group Roles

Discussion Facilitator:
Your role is to guide the group discussion and make sure that everyone has the chance to participate.

Scribe:
Your job is to record the ideas and comments your group members share.

Timekeeper:
You will keep track of how much time has passed and help keep the discussion moving along.

Encourager:
Your role is to motivate and support your group members.

Making Meaning with Words

Word	My Definition	My Sentence
bitter (p. 23)		
dodged (p. 31)		
greedy (p. 9)		
precious (p. 7)		
pummeled (p. 34)		
refreshing (p. 22)		
scrumptious (p. 6)		
selfish (p. 18)		
stumbled (p. 31)		
uneven (p. 35)		

Build Knowledge Across 10 Topic Strands

Lexile 420L–790L

Government and Citizenship

Character

Life Science

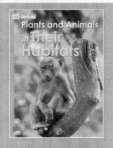

Point of View

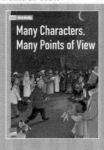

Technology and Society

Theme

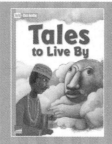

History and Culture

Earth Science

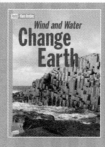

Economics

Physical Science

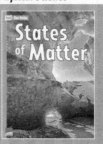

Benchmark
UNIVERSE.COM

BENCHMARK EDUCATION COMPANY

Grade 2 • Unit 6

ISBN 978-1-4900-9186-0

9 781490 091860